OCEANS ALIVE

Puffer Fish

by Colleen Sexton

BELLWETHER MEDIA • MINNEAPOLIS, MN

Note to Librarians, Teachers, and Parents:

Blastoff! Readers are carefully developed by literacy experts and combine standards-based content with developmentally appropriate text.

Level 1 provides the most support through repetition of high-frequency words, light text, predictable sentence patterns, and strong visual support.

Level 2 offers early readers a bit more challenge through varied simple sentences, increased text load, and less repetition of high-frequency words.

Level 3 advances early-fluent readers toward fluency through increased text and concept load, less reliance on visuals, longer sentences, and more literary language.

Level 4 builds reading stamina by providing more text per page, increased use of punctuation, greater variation in sentence patterns, and increasingly challenging vocabulary.

Level 5 encourages children to move from "learning to read" to "reading to learn" by providing even more text, varied writing styles, and less familiar topics.

Whichever book is right for your reader, Blastoff! Readers are the perfect books to build confidence and encourage a love of reading that will last a lifetime!

This edition first published in 2008 by Bellwether Media.

Library of Congress Cataloging-in-Publication Data
Sexton, Colleen A., 1967–
  Puffer fish / By Colleen Sexton.
    p. cm. — (Blastoff! readers: Oceans alive)
Summary: "Simple text and full color photographs introduce beginning readers to puffer fish. Developed by literacy experts for students in kindergarten through third grade"—Provided by publisher.
  Includes bibliographical references and index.
  ISBN-13: 978-1-60014-173-7 (hardcover : alk. paper)
  ISBN-10: 1-60014-173-0 (hardcover : alk. paper)
  1. Puffers (Fish)–Juvenile literature. I. Title.

  QL638.T32S49 2008
  597'.64–dc22   2007040278

Contents

Most puffer fish swim in warm ocean waters. Many live near **coral reefs**.

4

There are more than 120 different kinds of puffer fish.

Some puffer fish are as small as your hand.

Others are longer than
your arm.

Some puffer fish have stripes or spots on their skin. Some are very colorful.

Puffer fish have thick, rough skin. They do not have **scales** like other fish.

gills

Puffer fish breathe through **gills**.

fins

Puffer fish move their **fins**
and tail to swim.

Puffer fish eat clams, corals, sponges, and other animals.

Puffer fish have four teeth.
They use their teeth to
crush their food.

Sharks, sea snakes, and other **predators** hunt puffer fish.

Puffer fish have **poison** in their bodies. Some predators can die if they eat a puffer fish.

A puffer fish can also scare predators. It opens its mouth wide and gulps water.

Its body gets bigger and bigger. Its skin stretches.

Soon a puffer fish is almost round. **Spines** stick out from some puffer fish's bodies.

The spines are hidden in their skin until they puff up.

The puffer fish looks big and scary now. The predator may stop chasing the puffer fish.

Then the puffer fish can escape.

Glossary

coral reef—a structure in the ocean made of the skeletons of small ocean animals called corals

fins—flaps on a fish's body used for moving, steering, and stopping in the water

gills—openings on a puffer fish that it uses to breathe; gills move oxygen from the water to the fish's blood.

poison—a substance that can kill or harm a person or animal

predator—an animal that hunts other animals for food

scales—small, hard plates that cover the bodies of many kinds of fish

spines—a hard, sharp part on an animal or plant

To Learn More

AT THE LIBRARY

Foley, Cate. *Find the Fish*. New York: Children's Press, 2000.

Pfeffer, Wendy. *What's It Like to Be a Fish?* New York: HarperCollins, 2000.

Rake, Jody Sullivan. *Puffer Fish*. Mankato, Minn.: Pebble Books, 2007.

Sander, Sonia. *Rainbow Fish: Puffer Cries Shark*. New York: HarperCollins, 2003.

ON THE WEB

Learning more about puffer fish is as easy as 1, 2, 3.

1. Go to www.factsurfer.com

2. Enter "puffer fish" into search box.

3. Click the "Surf" button and you will see a list of related web sites.

With factsurfer.com, finding more information is just a click away.

Index

The images in this book are reproduced through the courtesy of: Steven Hunt/Getty Images, front cover; Raymond Connetta; p. 4; WaterFrame/Alamy p. 5; Norbert Wu/Getty Images, p. 6; Carlos Villoch/imagequestmarine.com, p. 7; Carlos Villoch/imagequestmarine.com, pp. 8-9; Raymond Connetta, p. 10; blickwinkel/Alamy, p. 11; Reinhard Dirscherl/Alamy, p. 12; David Fleetham/Alamy, p. 13; Richard Herrmann/Getty Images, pp. 14-15; David Fleetham/Alamy, p. 16 ; Steven Hunt/Getty Images, p. 17; David Fleetham/Alamy, p. 18; Steven Hunt/Getty Images, p. 19; Mark Conlin/V&W/imagequestmarine.com, pp. 20-21.